Cultivating Weeds:
Losing Myself in the Garden

Megan Baldrige

Happy Garden
Poetry

♡ *Megan*

Acknowledgments for Previously Published Poems

Coronavirus Day Seven; The Save-My Baby-Fruit Pantoum; The Skinks;
The Miller Moths and Me; Social Distancing With My Daughter's Dog;
This is a Mother Squash Lullaby, This is a Pumpkin Eulogy; The Seed;
Thanks to This Year's Garden; Ode to a Stuffed Poblano Green Chile
appeared in Of Pandemic, Politics & Pumpkin
(Poetry Playhouse Publications, 2020)

Holes Dug by His Holiness; Someone Tell the Neighborhood Birds;
Dogs Who Love the Garden; The Humungous, Scary Five-Foot Gopher Snake
in the Backyard
appeared in Cedro, The Dog Who Served His Backyard With Distinctio
(Poetry Playhouse Publications, 2017)

Wannabe Inside Moths; Thirsty Moths
appeared in Knitigating Circumstances
(Poetry Playhouse Publications, 2019)

A Public Service Announcement from the Sacred Datura Sestina;
The Lament of the Sacred Datura Sestina
appeared in Rolling Sixes Sestinas An Albuquerque Poetry Anthology
(Poetry Playhouse Publications, 2016)

ISBN: 9798459756029

This book is dedicated to all you gardeners who make the world bloom, especially to Diego, my gifted, hard-working gardener son who helps me, challenges me, sometimes humors me, makes me laugh.
And I am dedicating this book to my nephew Gardner Murray, just because.

Cultivating Weeds: Poems about Losing Myself in the Garden

Fourteen years ago, I bought a deserted desert backyard surrounding a house near the Rio Grande. First I moved into the house, then began to explore its six dirt areas: there were big shady cottonwood and elm trees and a wall for security, but the rest of the "garden" was a fixer-up project: a half-acre of sunburned grass, yucca, tumbleweeds, neighborhood weeds.

Since then, every year, I've worked on that garden. I've added humus and compost to the sometimes sandy, sometimes caliche desert soil; I've planted a variety of shrubs, trees, flowers and vegetables. Some plants have flourished for years, others for mere hours. Every winter, when no one was watching, many supposedly staunch perennials (like blanketflower or hollyhocks) passed on and disappeared, victims of drought, sun, aphids, rabbits, neglect or too much attention.

If I liked a plant, like blanketflower, even one that had failed in one or two places, I kept trying to find the sweet spot where it might flourish; likewise, every year I tried out new plants. That is to say, new plants to me and new plants to my garden. My goal was to plant a green and beautiful living tapestry that worked as a barrier to bindweed, foxtail grass and neighborhood weeds that still claimed ownership of my land. After many failures, some successes, my confidence as a gardener has grown.

A new garden built atop of tumbleweed takes a village of helpers. Along the way, my son Diego, Tony, Sienna, Eric, Steve, Ben, Toni, Sam, Tomlyn, Mick, Florian, Jake, Curtis, and Tomas have assisted with a patio, raised beds, murals, paths, annual planting, watering, weeding, fruit trees, rain dances. My black lab patrolled the yard and amended the soil with rawhide scraps.

I am a gardener who also likes to write poetry, so the cultivation of this garden has yielded poems. Here are a few about the plants that have my house surrounded and me captivated.

Megan Baldrige
August, 2021

Welcome, Spring!

They Show Up for Work in the Summer

The Mouthy Consumers

Winter Thoughts

Welcome Spring

Coronavirus Day Seven

This virus
separating
friend from friend,
grandmother from family,
one from another,

cannot keep the
plum tree
from singing,
"Spring is here!!"

The Save-My-Baby-Fruit Pantoum

The morbid April frost slunk in, to steal apricots, cherries, plums.
My old sheets, a sleeping bag, moving blankets, tarps,
     volunteered to protect cherry trees.
Sprinklers joined the brigade coating plum trees with ice.
For two nights we held vigil, me in bed; them, outside,
     fighting the invisible enemy.

My old sheets, a sleeping bag, moving blankets tarps,
     volunteered to protect cherry trees
Ice locked up tiny fruits with the promise of staycation, later in May.
For two nights we held vigil, me in bed; them, outside,
     fighting the invisible enemy.
Later the temperature rose slowly; I slowly rose to survey damage.

Ice locked up tiny fruits with the promise of staycation, later in May.
Pockmarked surfaces, tattooed tiny fruit, some dried up, others succulent.
Later, the temperature rose slowly; I rose slowly to survey damage;
the freeze selectively took some lives, spared others.

Pockmarked surfaces, tattooed tiny fruit, some dried up, others succulent.
We are inspired by late snowstorms, ice, impediment.
The freeze selectively took some lives, spared others;
the invisible enemy is on the march; spring is here.

We are inspired by late snowstorms, ice, impediment:
Sprinklers joined the brigade coating plum trees with ice;
the invisible enemy is on the march; spring is here.
The morbid April frost slunk in to steal baby apricots, cherries, plums.

*The April, 2020 freeze got the baby fruit, after all, despite my son's and my best efforts.
I didn't fit my son Diego into this form (because I was concentrating on the apricots)
but he was the architect of our moving-blanket tenting project. Thanks, Diego. You
deserve to be bigger than a footnote.

My Desert Toad, the Shy Cousin of Basho's Frog

In the desert where I live,
buried under an iris bed,
toads await birth.

Desert toads estivate,
bury themselves during summer heat,
to emerge from wet dirt after it rains.

They will never
be famous like Basho's frog
whose haiku splash—

the plop of frog into pond—
is still heard
around the world.

After it rains,
my toad surfaces
to look for a slick of mud,

some flies,
a damp place
to call home.

He hides from me,
so I cannot
write a haiku

immortalizing
his soundless jump
into cracked clay.

The Humongous Scary Five-Foot Gopher Snake in the Backyard

A motionless snake in the backyard.
The motionless snake appeared dead.

The dead snake, rubber?
The rubber snake, a practical joke?
The joke really lifeless?

The lifeless snake a facsimile of a real rattler?
The facsimile
not moving?
Or did I just see it
twitch?

A snake *probably* no longer moving
in the backyard.
WHAT IS IT DOING THERE?
Two puncture wounds on its chest look familiar,
like my dog's canine teeth.

My dog disavows knowledge
of these wounds,
of this snake.
My dog has been snake-proofed
at obedience school.

A snake-proofed dog is scared of snakes.
My supposedly
scared-of-snakes dog
feigns ignorance
of our backyard snake.

But he doggedly
shares this thought:
we do not want to approach
the lifeless, rubber, facsimile of a rattlesnake!
—just in case.

The Garden is Paved with Good Intentions

Last year's carrots too hairy to eat
lie beneath the surface of this year's garden.

So do the beets
infested by worms;

the cicada carcasses
that once played in an orchestra;

last summer's gaillardia
that disappeared down under;

the end-of-the-season
flea-bitten arugula leaves;

the sheep manure amendment
that stayed clumpy;

the millions of seeds
awaiting their moment in the sun;

the grass roots that refused
to be discouraged;

the front page of the Albuquerque Journal
escaped into vegetable bed;

the elm seedlings that self-started
and were torn out, then buried in the ground
by an elm-opposed weeder.

Spring Haiku

Thunder grumbles south
echoing madness, leaving
gentle rain behind

Wild wind tosses rain,
dandelions parachute down
reseed the lawn

The Skinks

Before the pandemic
I yielded the garden to the lizards
and skinks.

They, in turn, politely
scurried away,
whenever I walked outside.

But in April, I took it all back:
the garden, the back closet,
the sewing machine, the unfinished projects.

Especially
the
garden.

And the skinks
are
puzzled

when I'm home at nine am,
at noon, at three, five, seven,
rustling around their tierra.

This covid season,
I am putting more seeds into their turf,
taking more weeds out,

controlling
the garden
more.

The skinks watch skeptically,
making bets
on my commitment.

They rush off the garden path,
give way
in false deference.

They rustle,
swish into shrubbery,
skidaddle,

sigh more,
off stage,
in their sashaying way.

The lizards know
this garden
is theirs.

When I get the vaccine,
I will again occupy their garden
part-time.

*I kept reading about the impact of Coronavirus-sequestering on dogs and cats, but I wondered about the garden lizards and skinks.

The Compost Pile

Oh, wormy compost pile:
you have brought
robins to the garden,

and fly larvae
cradled amid onion skins
and putrid potato peels.

Your swampiness malingers
in a bin brewing bruised broccoli
and beetles.

Some larvae love a bog,
thrive amid mildewed moldered muck,
atop islands of coffee grounds.

Others avoid burial;
instead, migrate
from one zip code to another.

During the summer the buried bunch bursts up,
bursts down, eats sideways, diagonally
like a mad Rube Goldberg machine.

Generations of earthworms
have never left the comfort
of their compost pile.

Likewise, their children,
grandchildren
never look far for dinner.

Behind Every Successful Lettuce…

Behind every successful
lettuce,

lives a March gardener
who remembered to order seeds;

lies an April gardener
who remembered to plant seeds;

lives a May gardener
who remembers to water seeds;

lie one thousand-and-one weed seeds
who bask in that water,

ready to knock out
that precious, putative, presumptive, pampered pet lettuce.

The Miller Moths and Me

I may not have told you this:
I am sequestering
with five thousand Miller moths.

I hope it's ok, Governor Michelle Lujan Grisham,
I wanted to be home alone;
then, unannounced, the rowdy neighbors showed up.

They love
to emerge from the hollow place
in the exterior door frame, at dinnertime.

Three thousand of them
have flown out of one door
in this season of Miller moths.

They live like James Dean:
bigly dying, already dead,
or very alive, in a fluttering way.

They dance, then expire,
on my pillow, on every window sill
in the bathtub, on kitchen counters.

As I sequester at home,
the divas get the attention
they have always wanted.

A porch light has finally been replaced.
I am home to attend to their antics
every night.

When I walk inside,
they bum rush the door,
ready to languish,

to walk through
the famed tunnel of light
on their passage out.

They Show Up for Work in the Summer

Over-Elmed by June

I've been awaiting you,
dear friend June:
you who woo me,
make me swoon.

Sashay over, show me shimmer;
Let's bust hot moves, let's get glimmer.
Give me sun, I'll show you skin;
Let's open doors, stay light late, let fresh air in.

But, I beg you, my promiscuous,
permissively pollinating
Junebug mistress:
enough elm mischief!

That seedy elm gang has my yard discovered,
my just-watered vegetables covered
by tufts of diaphonous stuff
fluttering in a hover of shifting grifty tough fluff.

Every June
I'm over-elmed,
--unsettled, rattled, locked in battle, not ready to coddle,
ready to throttle the elms and you.

So, dear June, no more elm pollination,
nor elm-baby procreation;
no more elm seeding, nor elm feeding.
I can't be twenty-four/seven million-elm weeding.

June, repeat after me:
I will no longer reseed the Siberian elm tree!

Gild the Lily

No need to gild
the lily with fragrance, paint or glitter.

The lily,
perfect as it is.

Yet gild the lily
with your attention.

Sit and admire a maroon-striped orange lily
for five minutes.

Become bewitched
by its beauty.

Unendangered Weeds

Hunkering survivalists bunker in my garden
flaunt, taunt, haunt me
as I walk the backyard.

Grab-hearted,
caliche-clinging foxtail grass
circles my house,

threatens take-over,
slices the hand that
weeds it.

Bindweed,
unapologetically
UNannihilated,

claims my dirt,
from its cave garden
under the sunflower roots.

Its tentacles choke
backyard rocks
in spools of roots,

chase hints
of water
into tight places.

Bindweed is here, and there,
and over here,
and over there.

It is born again every time
I dig up
a tiny sacrificial tendril,

then leave behind
the ancestral root
it sprang from.

Elm seeds warn me
"No vacation for you
this summer.

"You never know when the monsoons
will return to give us new life,
new life, new life, new life, new life, new life, new life.

"We never take a day off;
our sacred rite is to rule
your yard.

"We were here first,
chorus the foxgrass,
the bindwind, the Russian thistle.

"Even if you rise at dawn
and come after us
with sharpened spades,

we never give up
our roots
our gnarled cojones, our underground brains."

Like a poodle
that dares howl at coyotes
I'm outgunned.

My coquettish
petunias
will not ruffle for long.

Yes, the bindweed
will wrap me in its arms

when I return to the garden someday—
as ashy dirt.

Two Coneflower Tales

1
Sometimes a purple coneflower
waltzes into your life
for a few days of
extreme flowering—
in a summer of orange marigolds and redhot poker,

so you can admire
the strong, perfect petals,
be mesmerized by the splash of fresh color.

2
The front yard coneflower
and the backyard coneflower
somehow
picked

today
to turn up the heat,
explode.

But how
did they tell each other
that today is the day?

The Hollyhocks

A dusky purple hollyhock
greets me
next to the driveway.

Its saucer-sized
flowers
are open this week,

as they were
all
last week.

This wild hollyhock seeded itself
in a desert strip of tar
surrounded by sand,

pushed
branches out
like a multi-trunked tree.

I am a gardener:
this wild hollyhock flourishes
on my neglect.

I am a gardener:
I plant, water, tend
four other hollyhocks limping through July heat.

I have wired them against the rabbits
planted them in rich soil,
watered thirsty them.

I am a gardener:
My flowers are pallid
scrawny, rabbit-chewed.

I am a gardener
needing to learn the art
of Not-gardening.

A Public Service Announcement from the Sacred Datura Sestina

Flower children,
Don't pick me!
Please don't eat my seeds and leaves!
Let me not be disturbed.
As poison is my only defense,
my beauty is deadly.

The first swallow of my seeds may not be deadly.
You will wish to die; instead, your brain becomes childish;
and you will forever defend
your increasing disabilities to insurance companies, so, to me,
you will be disturbed
by a decision to eat a few leaves.

I agree my flowers and leaves
are beautiful, but, remember, deadly
leaving you disturbed
and, if you survive to have children,
they will also be disturbed and blame me.
And that is my only defense.

Which, in my own defense,
leaves
me
some peace, as I am a damsel deadly
who wants to be loved by botanists and children
but not to derange and disturb.

If my garden is disturbed
I will try to wilt, in my defense,
so that your children
will not want to eat my flowers and leaves.
The legacy of being deadly
is that, provoked, the only survivor is me.

Don't pick me!
Do not disturb.
I am beautiful and deadly.
That, dear judges, is my defense,
so leave
me behind, hippies, dreamers and flower children.

Deadly me: Consume me,
turn childish, be disturbed.
You are warned: I defend myself, so best leave me in peace.

The Lament of the Sacred Datura Sestina

My friends call me jimsonweed;
my fans insist I'm royal, a Sacred Datura.
Do not publicize where I live;
allow me to humbly be:
a virginal blossom basking at sunrise,
who tries to stay out of the limelight.

Georgia O'Keefe thrust me into limelight:
a shy jimsonweed
facing the setting sunset
of my own beauty as sacred datura,
beloved patroness of a few local bees,
a beauty who simply wants to live.

I want to live
simply, out of the limelight
and only be
a humble jimsonweed,
a Sacred Datura
opening gorgeously at sunrise.

Idolize me if you must, especially at sunrise,
when I do my interviews live.
Consider me first and foremost datura,
if you insist I bask in the limelight.
Don't call me a jimsonweed,
rather a diva datura beloved by bees.

Who doesn't like to be
admired at sunrise?
Don't forget that I'm mostly NOT jimsonweed.
I may wilt a bit in the sun, but I'm lively
in limelight.
My Latin name is Datura Wrightii, aka Sacred Datura.

That's D-A-T-U-R-A, Datura.
Of the sacred Datura family I be.
Especially lovely in limelight,
I blush with my own beauty at sunrise.
I look more alive
as Datura than as jimsonweed.

Remember it's Datura not jimsonweed.
Beware of how beautiful I am alive, unpicked.
You may paint me, but, please, only at sunrise or in the limelight.

Way to Go, Sunlight

Sunlight needs an Aztec warrior
every thousand years,
or so,
to lose a ball game
and donate a heart,

to feed the eternal
blasted
everlasting
drought-proof
sunshine.

Sunlight,
ladle out your beams generously.
Don't believe everything
you read about yourself in fanzines;
you don't need a press agent.

Who nourishes
sunshine
when Apollo is holed up in a Greek temple?
when my stamp collection
is heavy on grey postwar Hungary?

Sunlight
just needs
a little
boost
to horizon hop.

Bring it on,
turn it up,
sunshine, oh sunburn,
which, on me,
just burns baby burns.

Discretely "Chillaxing"

Years ago
a teenaged son banned me
from using the word "chillax."
I was not millennial enough, he puffed.

Since then I've been *secretly* "chillaxing" in the garden—
describing that moment
when the weeding is done,
so I find a cool corner in the backyard.

With an icy drink,
in the hands of a good novel,
"chillaxing" becomes
me.

I gaze around beds
where weeds
used to roam
and "chillax, chillax, chillax."

Serendipity You Can Bank On

Sacred datura, hollyhock,
sunflower, euphorbia, mullein—

they are the serendipities
of my garden:

the hippy
plants

who show up
on their own every year.

Plant them: they languish,
are stunted, dwarfed.

Let them plant themselves:
they flourish, gigantically.

"Remember me?
I'm YOUR weed," they claim.

They clamorously appoint themselves,
steal the garden's worst real estate.

After monsoon rains,
you can watch them

show up,
show off.

Summer Haiku

Feeder hummingbird,
too fat for desert flowers
pride of our garden

Follow snail slime
under blooming lavender
surely snails can smell

Along milkweed pods,
orange grid of aphid eggs
awaits birth, breakfast

A toddler beats us
to garden's red tomatoes,
leaves us hard green ones

Ode to Last Year's Hose

Last year,
flowing
with water,
a humble hose
saved me,
the gaillardias and hollyhocks
from death by sunstroke.

This helpful hose
tripped me
when I forgot to water thirsty tomatoes,
whispered to me,
at night,
mid-garden
up to my bedroom.

"Turn on the faucet"
I heard blowing
in the wind
when I awoke at night,
so hot I dreamt
I was chased by
fireworks.

Last July
my supple assistant
worked overtime,
uncomplaining of heat prostration,
being run over by cars,
trapped under rocks,
sequestered during the rains.

This hose coupled well
with its faucet,
hooked up
with a diva nozzle,
never minding
when the trigger
stuck on flood.

Underappreciated,
overextended,
pushed, pulled,
stretched,
but never laid
low
by being underfoot.

Last fall this tired hero
napped in the corner
in the lambs' ears bed
in relaxed repose.
Yes, last year's hose
deserved a retirement
on a pedestal in the garage.

But, unfaithfully,
I uncoupled
our partnership,
when I unscrewed
last year's hose from the wall
and replaced
it with this year's hose.

I laid last year's hose to rest
amidst glass shards
at the recycling bin on Edith;
In a half hour,
my betrayed friend disappeared,
never again to be fondled
by me, Judas.

Then I met
this year's hose
who insisted
I buy its one-year warranty
before it agreed
to leave the
Lowe's nursery shelf.

It refused
to be hailed
as hose,
wanted to be known
as "neverkinkmax",
but sprawled kinkily,
nonetheless.

This year's hose erupted
in a geyser
on its first day of work,
a hot Saturday in June.
Was the leak from heat,
or having to
work weekends?

This disobedient hose
refused to lay flat,
didn't like the faucet
and wanted to hook up with whom
it wanted to hook up,
but definitely not
with last year's nozzle.

My lawyer
advises I go no
further with this poem
of defamation
about this year's
crappy, low-quality,
trumped-up hose.

The Seed

The seed turned into
a hollowed-out pumpkin
with a grim death stare.

Thanks to This Year's Garden

Thank you to this year's garden—
the orange cherry tomatoes
that refuse to stop,

the big tomatoes
that are still turning to red,

the green tomatoes
that ripen to green,

and the big blue pumpkin
that said "No Way" to the squash bugs.

Ode to a Stuffed Poblano Green Chile

Who could bear to bread a poblano chile
pinched from the garden,
then freshly roasted before it rained last night?

Instead, its folds are stuffed,
some with blue cheese,
some with sautéed oyster mushrooms.

Shall I go on
about how to treat a fresh, lusty poblano
that deserves immortality,

but, instead,
will be eaten,
with gusto?

The Southwest Bosque Guide to Hillary's Cracking the Glass Ceiling at the Democratic Convention 2016

The solipsism of sunflowers:
"We don't care,
as long as it's sunny."

Yells and yippees
from the Texas red yucca:
"You go get em girl!"

The buzz of the beeplant:
"Bernie's people have you surrounded,
and they're not in a good mood."

The remorselessness
of the Russian thistle:
"Let's just wiki-leak the DNC."

The quandary of the kiss-me-quick:
"Bill can have a corner office;
but make sure there's a camera in <u>every</u> corner."

The guile of the puncture vine:
"Let's give Hillary one good night!
Before she is deflated."

The sensibility of the smooth amaranth:
"What did Hillary ever do
for the silvery minnow?"

The Mouthy Consumers

A Mother Squash Bug Lullaby, A Pumpkin Eulogy

This is a song
for all my squash bug eggs
hidden
on the Jarrahdale pumpkin plant.

You are
infinite
in number—
on July 20.

Dining on new buds
at dusk,
I spy you—
my newly hatched.

Tiny balls of sticks,
or two-day-old porcelain
robin's egg blue bits
with six roving legs.

You drill blossoms,
share thirst
for sweet sap
of pumpkin flower.

Upon which stem or leaf did I lay you?
There are so many of you.
We glance at each other, across petals,
me mom-proud: there are so many of you!

You,
many daughters—
all born loving
pumpkins.

This is a lullaby about multitude.
This is a lullaby about plentitude.
This is a lullaby about plethora.
This is a lullaby about profusion.

This is a ballad about coverage,
overage, overachieving,
achieving success,
excess, succession.

This is an ode to pumpkins withering on the vine,
the ones that never had a chance,
whirring, stuttering,
shuddering, shuttering.

This is a eulogy about
one garden dream
that fed on another.

*thanks to Joanne Arnott's *Song About* for suggesting this poem's form

Wannabe-Inside Moths

The clothes moths
hiding in the front door wreath
assail me.

I spy a little flutter-wiggle
as they move from the wreath, push-shoving
toward the door I am opening.

They almost escape into my house—
a sanctuary
full of wool.

But I block them,
quickly shut the door
before they can mob and rob me.

They are small moths
with hungry stomachs
and short lives.

Thirsty Moths

I am trying to take care of my wool moths:
After I shower in the morning,
I leave water for them in the tub.

"Free water for thirsty moths!"
I announce
to my closet full of moths.

"Perchance you'd like
to swim in a porcelain pool,
not eat my sweater."

In the afternoon I am greeted
by lifeless clothes moths
in my bathtub.

So sorry, moths:
I forgot
to leave you a life raft.

Ha ha.

The Squash Bug Battle Played Out in Heroic Scale in my Backyard

The squash bug squadron
just flew into town,
unannounced,
apparently
summering
in my garden,
again.

They,
I,
each enjoy,
the very same real estate
which I believe to be
MY garden,
not theirs.

I,
outnumbered,
practice
dominance
with scissors and hose,
during morning meet-
and greet sessions.

You know
how it goes
with hillbilly neighbors:
the summer population
grows
exponentially,
every half hour.

The survivors
feed,
fatten,
thicken, procreate
as I wean out
their lesser
brethren.

I try persuasion:
"Why my garden?
Why not Susan's, next door:
she is not a vigilante!
"Anyway,
don't you need
more sleep—like the ladybugs?"

I ask nosy questions,
'Why so much sex?
Too many nymphs
is a burden: twenty is okay,
two thousand
in two weeks:
totally too many.

"Have you heard
about the lemmings?
what happened to them
at the cliff
when they overdid
the kid thing?"

But squash bugs
love their big families;
three generations gather to eat
my delicious blossoms
free-range, rent-free.
The adults play peekaboo
scurry and scamper, dart and dodge.

The battalion
lines up
its eggs,
squarely rooted
in sixteens
and twenty-fives,
on the underside of leaves.

I squish those eggs,
so easy to destroy,
but miss hidden ones becoming nymphs
who plummet to dirt
when cornered,
never giving up
without a high-speed chase scene.

The nymphs
have a moment
of transparent porcelain
blue beauty,
when they are a day old,
fragile
from egg escape.

They start dining
on my baby
blossoms,
then turn into
the ugliest
of all bugs.

My squash blossoms
die exhausted,
wasted,
foreshortened lives.
and I grumpily
buy zucchini
from a grocer.

The Rabbit and I

"He's thirsty," says the irrigation guy
showing me holes in an underground water tube
spurting gusts of water.
Something says rabbit teeth to him.

"Thirsty my foot,"
I say,
pointing to the Rio Grande,
visible, nearby.

That rabbit
is living
next to the second longest
river in America.

Don't post-millennial rabbits
smell water anymore?
feel water in their bones,
want to drink at riverbanks?

I used to like Easter rabbits,
chocolate bunnies,
even bad
little Peter Rabbit.

This rabbit family
and I will be wrangling
water rights
on shared land.

I am buying a hose
to water that rabbit,
his fraternal twins, his cousins, his village,
his New Mexican clan hovering nearby.

If the rabbit
takes over my irrigation system,
that hose will be handy
for hand-watering the garden.

Dogs Who Love the Garden

Few gardeners are canines;
few canines are real gardeners.

A gifted puppy might unintentionally
scratch up a weed or two,
but never all the tumbleweeds he planted
last year in a joyous burst of excavation.

Burying his bone,
that digger helpfully
aerates the soil
around the trumpet vine.

Looking for that bone in the compost pile
he stirs up beneficial enzymes,
but not without strewing
half composted bok choy over garden paths.

While trailing a human gardener,
your average canine will stand on the furrow,
right where you have just planted
exquisite heirloom tomatoes

and quizzically look into your eyes.
A not-irresistible
"Do you still love me,
while I am standing on the seedlings?" sort of look.

A dog-loving gardener responds:
"I love you, I love the garden,
but I don't love you IN the garden."

Someone Tell the Neighborhood Birds

Someone tell the neighborhood birds
that the fierce dog
who protected his backyard with passion
has left us.

It is safe for them
to visit
the bird feeder
once again.

Holes Dug By His Holiness

The canine backyard renovation
stopped holefully incomplete,
when the architect,
my digging dog, died.

Now, seven pounds of rawhide bones—
buried in secret places—
could be sold as scrap
and holes filled in,

yet it is unholy
to undo
the hard work
of a good dog.

Social Distancing with My Daughter's Dog

Someone's been licking my foot brace, again.
it's dampish, warm to touch in the morning.

I appreciate my daughter's dog's
—my grand-dog's—concern for my broken ankle.

Sniff away,
Canela.

Yesterday we celebrated
a victory of our co-sequestration with ankle injuries.

Your cone was removed,
duct tape reinforced on your ankle bandage.

But by noon, the tape was breached;
the cone went back on.

We
commiserated.

Admit it, you social distance better
with a plastic cone on.

Is it metaphor when I see you and me
limping through a backyard garden that needs weeding?

Is it The Road?
Me playing Viggo Mortensen, you as my son.

No, in fact, your Dad, my son-in-law
is watering the zinnias

while you and I walk in circles,
admiring the flights of moths and hummingbirds.

The watering
reminds me

that my people and their rescue dog
moved in when I broke my ankle, needed help.

Out came home-made pad thai,
breakfast on the sofa, help watering.

Not isolation,
not social distancing.

Instead, extra bottom sniffs
and body slams.

Winter Thoughts

January

Time
for recuperation:

a vintage gardener
rests, reads garden catalogues;

last summer's garden
hibernates.

Winter Haiku

In the cottonwood,
egret awaits winter snow
in the big v-crook

Grey sky cloud curtain
a rare New Mexico morn,
monolithic calm

Japanese Garden Sestina

A Japanese gardener rakes curves
around islands of moss-covered rocks,
as my feet meander.
Here no flowers swagger
to distract a subdued garden formula.
Except, rules oblivious, a butterfly zigzags.

In delight at that slow-motion zigzag.
my eyes are pulled to pine curves—
branches pruned into cloud forms.
What is the symbol for this rock:
Is it turtle or crane? No, I want to swagger
to my own beat of meaning from meandering.

When a gardening poet tries to writefully meander,
like winter thunder, slinging zigzags
of metaphors to create swag,
the words can thud, curdle, curve
around themselves, halted by stoic rocks
resisting verbal formulas.

Many years ago, I was bedazzled by fifteen rock forms
at the Ryanji Garden where I came meandering.
Each craggy icon beautiful in a rocky
way, my eye delighted zigzagging
around miniature pinnacles, ripples and curves
of raked gravel garden, subtly swaggering.

But the beauty was undone by modern swagger:
the multilingual loudspeaker declaiming the meaning of each form.
A continuous loop explained the rocks, the curves.
As my mind no longer thrilled to meander,
a headache took me zigzagging
away from contemplation of rocks.

That day, I left behind the rocks.
Too much swagger
left me praying for silence, zigzagging
from a garden where words hid forms.
The wonder which comes from meandering
dissolved at my feet in gravel, dusty dead end, not inviting curve.

Remembering zigzags of Japanese gardens I have known,
I love to follow curving paths that swagger with surprise.
Or with familiar forms delighting a meandering wanderer.

The Same Sun

Will today's sun that blisters
backyard rocks
return tomorrow: the *same* sun?

Will that friendly sun
still tap my shoulder warmly,
announcing, "I'm here."

Will the same sun rest
on the bedroom floor tomorrow,
take a nap with me after lunch?

Will a hotter sun
return to set sunflower stalks
on fire?

Will a crueler sun
invade the house,
burn the napping baby's cheek?

Will that different sun
steal water
from farmers' acequias?

Siphon it sunward,
away from rivers, lakes, fish, frogs,
away from farms?